OSWESTRY TO
WHITCHURCH
and the
WREXHAM BRANCH

Vic Mitchell and Keith Smith

MP Middleton Press

Front cover: Bound for Ellesmere on 28th June 1958 is 0-4-2T no. 1423, a popular class on the route from Wrexham. It was photographed there, at Central Station, platform 3. (G.Adams/M.J.Stretton coll.)

Back cover upper: The 1400 class 0-4-2Ts were faithful servants on the Wrexham branch and no. 1432 is seen leaving Bangor-on-Dee on 1st September 1962, ten days before the line closed. (Colour-Rail.com)

Back cover lower: In the early years of the 21st century, a display of assorted diesel locomotives was to be found outside the former Oswestry Locomotive & Carriage Works. However, this Andrew Barclay product of 1902 was petrol driven. (T.Heavyside)

THE AUTHORS

In 1981 the authors wrote Branch Lines to Midhurst and decided to have it published to coincide with the events they were arranging to mark the centenary of the opening of the Chichester to Midhurst line. It being rejected by several publishers as too parochial, Vic Mitchell decided to publish it himself under the imprint of Middleton Press, a move which resulted in a subsequent and ongoing series of albums, described recently as "Evolving the Ultimate Rail Encyclopedia". The index to stations now covers more than 100 pages on our website.

Vic and Keith would like to thank again all those who have offered encouragement and expressed their appreciation of the series, and in particular, those who have contributed so much material. They are seen below in front of a model of Midhurst LSWR terminus.

Vic Mitchell and Keith Smith

Published July 2010
ISBN 978 1 906008 81 9
© Middleton Press, 2010
Design Deborah Esher

Printed in the United Kingdom by
  Henry Ling Limited,
  at the Dorset Press,
  Dorchester, DT1 1HD

Published by
  Middleton Press
  Easebourne Lane
  Midhurst,
  West Sussex. GU29 9AZ
Tel: 01730 813169
Fax: 01730 812601
Email: info@middletonpress.co.uk
www.middletonpress.co.uk

CONTENTS

INDEX

ACKNOWLEDGEMENTS

We are very grateful for the assistance received from many of those mentioned in the credits, also to A.R.Carder, L.Crosier, G.Croughton, F.Hornby, J.B.Horne, D.K.Jones, P.J.Kelley, N.Langridge, B.Lewis, A.C.Mott, Mr D. and Dr S.Salter, L.Wass and in particular, our always supportive wives, Barbara Mitchell and Janet Smith.

I. Routes in the area in 1951, with the former GWR ones shown bold.

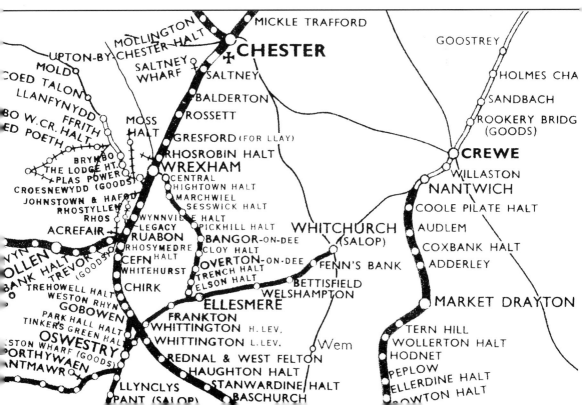

GEOGRAPHICAL SETTING

The Oswestry to Whitchurch route traverses undulating agricultural upland, mostly between 200 and 400ft above sea level. The branch to Wrexham dips below this to cross the Dee Valley, north of Bangor-on-Dee.

Most of the district overlies sandstones. These fringe the narrow coal measures, which stretch from Oswestry to Wrexham and beyond.

The Oswestry-Welshampton section, together with three miles west of Whitchurch, were built in Shropshire. Wrexham and Marchweil were in Denbighshire, while the remaining four stations were constructed in a detached part of Flintshire. Ironically the eastern end of the Cambrian Railways and also its headquarters at Oswestry, were in England.

The maps are to the scale of 25ins to 1 mile, with north at the top, unless otherwise stated.

Gradient Profile

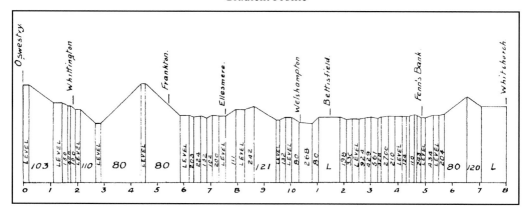

August 1939

HISTORICAL BACKGROUND

The Shrewsbury & Chester Railway was opened from Chester through Wrexham in 1846 and on through Whittington in 1848. It became part of the Great Western Railway in 1854. Oswestry gained a branch from it in 1848 and the route south thereof, to Welshpool, was opened in 1860 by the Oswestry & Newtown Railway.

Whitchurch received its first station when the London & North Western Railway opened between Shrewsbury and Crewe in 1858. Its line between Whitchurch and Chester came into use in 1872, but closed to passengers in 1957.

The Oswestry, Ellesmere & Whitchurch Railway opened between the latter two places on 4th May 1863 and on to Oswestry on 27th July 1864.

An Act of 25th July 1864 formed the Cambrian Railways and the OE&WR was one of four lines to be combined at that time. The CR operated the new route between Ellesmere and Wrexham from 2nd July 1895. It shared the 1887 terminus of the Wrexham, Mold & Connah's Quay Railway. This became Wrexham Central: the station was owned by the Great Central Railway from 1905 and thus the London & North Eastern Railway from 1923. The Wrexham & Ellesmere Railway became part of the GWR in 1922.

The CR became part of the GWR in 1922 and the LNWR formed the western area of the London Midland & Scottish Railway in 1923.

With the advent of nationalisation, all the GWR lines in the area became part of the Western Region of British Railways on 1st January 1948. The route was transferred to the London Midland Region on 17th June 1963 operationally, but officially on 1st January.

The route between Ellesmere and Wrexham Central closed to passengers on 10th June 1940 as a wartime economy measure, but it carried a heavy munitions traffic from local works. It reopened on 6th May 1946, but closed permanently on 10th September 1962. Oswestry to Whitchurch followed on 18th January 1965. Closure dates of the goods depots are given in the captions.

PASSENGER SERVICES

We look at train frequencies in the down (southward) direction on weekdays. There were no Sunday trains, except one at night, each way. Departure from Whitchurch was between 2.0 and 3.0am, the up one being at around 9.0pm from Oswestry. These night trains ran daily.

The train frequency grew from 5 to 8 in the 19th century and remained mostly at 8 until the end. There was often a Manchester through train.

The Ellesmere-Wrexham branch was consistent with 7 or 8 trains, weekdays only. A through service to Oswestry is mentioned in caption XI and shown in the accompanying timetable of 1899.

July 1899. Includes a through non-stop train from Wrexham to Oswestry.

ces:—London Road Sta., Manchester.]	WREXHAM and ELLESMERE.—Cambrian.																		
Fares cl. 3 cl.	Down.	mrn	mrn	mrn	aft	aft	aft	aft		Fares from Ellesmere. SINGLE. RETURN 1 cl. 3 cl. 1 cl. 3 cl.	Up.	mrn	mrn	mrn	aft	aft	aft	aft	aft
....	Wrexham (Central)......dep	7 0	8 15	9 55	12 5	1 35	5 55	6 30	9 15		Oswestry 347......dep	8 40	....	1140	1 50	2 55	5 25	....	9 40
....	Marchwiel ...	7 5	8 20	10 0	....	1 40	4 0	6 35	9 20		Whitchurch 346... "	8 25	1020	....	1 50	....	5 30	6 40	9 25
....	Bangor-on-Dee	7 13	8 28	10 8	....	1 48	4 8	6 43	9 28		Ellesmere ......dep	9 5	1055	12 5	2 20	3 15	5 55	7 15	10 5
....	Overton-on-Dee	7 20	8 35	1015	....	1 55	4 15	6 50	9 35		Overton-on-Dee	9 15	11 5	1215	2 30	3 25	6 5	7 25	1015
....	Ellesmere 346, 347... arr	7 30	8 46	1025	....	2 5	4 25	7 0	9 45		Bangor-on-Dee	9 21	1111	1221	2 36	3 31	6 11	7 31	1021
....	Whitchurch 347... arr	....	9 30	1157	....	2 39	5 10	....	1025		Marchwiel	9 30	1120	1228	2 45	3 40	6 20	7 40	1030
....	Oswestry 346...... "	7 58	9 15	1047	1240	2 35	6 8	7 28	1015		Wrexham (Cen.) 351, 40 arr	9 35	1125	1233	2 50	3 45	6 25	7 45	1035

July 1899

WHITCHURCH, OSWESTRY, ABERYSTWYTH, BARMOUTH, PWLLHELI, &c. Cambrian.

Offices—Oswestry. Gen. Man., C. S. Denniss. Sec., R. Brayne. Supt. of Line, W. H. Gough.

Down. Week Days. Sndys

Euston Station,	mrn	mrn	mrn	3 cl.	mrn	mrn	mrn	mrn	aft	mrn	aft	mrn	aft	aft	aft	aft	mrn	aft
LONDON 310 ....dep.	8 50					5 15		8 30						1215	2 15	5 30	8 50	
400 M'CHESTER (L.R.) "	12 0					8 35		1045				1150		3 30	4 45	7 2	12 0	
386 L'POOL (Lime St.) "	1155					8 15		1030				1210		3 25	4 35	7 0	1155	
CREWE 338 .... "	1 40					9 35		1149				1 20		4 05	5 40	8 45	1 40	
Whitchurch....dep.	2 25				8 25	1010	1020	1220		1 50				5 20	6 40	9 25	2 25	
Fenn's Bank	Sig.				8 32		1028			1 57				5 28	6 48	9 32	Sig.	
Bettisfield	Sig.				8 39	e	1036			2 5				5 36	6 56	9 39	Sig.	
Welshampton	Sig.				8 44		1040			2 9				Sig.	7 0	9 43	Sig.	
Ellesmere 348	2 55				7 40	8 57	1033	1050		2 17				5 50	7 10	9 57	2 55	
Frankton...[35, 40]	Sig.				7 45	9 2		1055		2 22				5 55	7 15	10 2	Sig.	
Whittington (H. Level)	Sig.				7 53	9 10	e	11 3		2 30				6 3	7 23	1010	Sig.	
Oswestry 45 ....arr.	3 15				7 58	9 15	1047	11 8	1250	2 35				6 8	7 28	1015	3 15	
356 M'CHESTER (Ex) dep							7 45		9 40			1045	1240	1	5 2	35	4 20	
354 L'POOL (Ldg. S.) "					6 0		8 0		1020			1150	1240	2	40	3	20 5 10	
Oswestry ....dep.	3 30				8 5		1053	Sig.	1255			2 40	3 45	5	0	6 15	7 35	6 15
Llynclys					8 13		Sig.					2 48	3 55	5	10	6 23	7 45	6 23
Pant					Sig.		Sig.					2 53		Sig.	7 50		Sig.	
Llanymynech { arr.	Sig.				8 18		11 5					2 52	4 3	5 17	6 24	7 54	6 20
348 { dep.	Sig.				8 20		11 6					2 54	4 3	5 20	6 30	7 57	6 35
Four Crosses					8 25		1110					Sig.	Stop	5 25	6 35	8 1	
Arddleen					Mn.									5 31			
Pool Quay	Sig.				8 35		1118					Sig.		5 37	6 43	8 10	6 42
Buttington 335	Sig.				8 40		1122					Sig.		5 42	6 53	8 16	6 48
Welshpool *....arr.	4 25				8 45		1127		1 20			3 13		5 50	6 59	8 22	6 55
34 LONDON (Pad.) dep.	6 50	d			1210	d			9 30		9 50		Stop	2 10			1210	
310 " (Euston) "	10 0	d				5 15			9 30		11 0	aft		2 35			1010	
35 BIRMINGHAM (SH) "	1033	d			6 0		8 30		12 4		1248	1 40		3 40			Sig.	
311 " (New St.) "	1142					7 20			1135		1225		3 cl.	3 35			1142	i
335 SHREWSBURY "	3 40				7 55		1020		1 20		2 42	3 20	aft	6 8			6 0	
Welshpool ....dep.	4 40		7 55		8 50		1135		1 25		2 20	3 25	4 20	5 30	7 20	8 30		
Forden			8 5		9 0		f						4 25	5 40	7 28	8 40		
Montgomery	4 51		8 10		9 4		1147		1 34		h		h	4 32	5 50	7 38	8 46		
Abermule 348			8 20		9 12		Sig.						4 42	6 0	7 48	8 53		
Newtown	5 8		8 30		9 26		12 7		1 52		h		3 50	4 54	6 10	7 53	9 10		
Moat Lane Jn. 348 arr.	5 16		Stop		9 36		1215		2 0		2 59		3 58	5 2	6 18	8 1	9 20		
LLANIDLOES 348 arr	5 50				1010		1245		3 12		3 12			5 27		8 45	9 45		
Moat Lane June...dep.	5 21				9 42		1220		2 3		2 52	3 35	4	5 7		8 10		7 48
Caersws	5 23				9 45		f						5 9		Sig.		7 51
Pontdolgoch					Sig.								5 14		8 4		7 54
Carno	5 33				9 56		fl						5 20		8 18		8 6
Llanbrynmair	5 42				1015		fl						5 32		8 16		8 16
Cemmes Road 354	5 53				1030		1 5			4 12		b		5 43		8 30		8 40
Machynlleth 349 arr.	6 1				1039		1 15		2 40		3 32	4 22	4 45	5 51	aft	8 55		8 45
Machynlleth dep	6 48		9 50	1042		1 20		2 48		3 35	4 24	4 50	5 55	6 55	9 0		8 45
Glandovey June..	8 55		1010	1055		1 28		2 57	3 18		4 35			7 10		
Glandovey	6 12	8 58		1013	k		1 40		3 21				6 3	7 13		
Ynyslas		9 10		1025	k			3 33				6 14	7 25		
Borth	6 25	9 14		1030	1115		1 55		b	3 37	b	4 50	b	6 20	7 30	9 25		
Llanfihangel		9 19		1037	k			3 44				k	7 36		
Bow Street	6 31	9 25		1042	k		2 15		3 50			6 35	7 41		
Aberystwyth 66	6 40	9 34	mrn	1055	1135		2 15	3 35	4 0	4 20	5 10	5 30	6 50	7 55	9 45		
Machynlleth ....dep.	6 15		7 40	Stop	7 50	Stop	1042		1 20		2 55		3 42	Stop	6 10	Stop		8 55
GlandoveyJune. { arr.			8 0		1050		1 28								6 18			
{ dep.				8 0		1055		1 40							6 23			
Aberdovey	6 35		8 15		11 9		1 54		b		b		b	6 47		9 18	
Towyn ‖ 351	6 43		8 25		1117		2 3		4 12		b			6 55		9 30	
Llwyngwril	6 55		8 40		1131		2 17							7 9		9 41	
Fairbourne			Sig.		Sig.		Sig.							Sig.		9 53	4 50
Barmouth Junction	7 5	mrn	8 53	mrn	1142		2 28		aft		aft	5 50	7 22		
Barmouth dep.	8 5	9 5	1015	1215		2 50		4 10	5 55		7 0		8 35			
Barmouth Junc.	8 10	9 16		1225		3 0		4 20	6 5		7 10		8 41			
Arthog	8 13	9 18		1228		3 4		4 23	6 8		7 13		8 44			
Penmaenpool	8 25	9 30	j	1242		3 15		4 35	6 20		7 25		8 55			
Dolgelley ‡ 48 arr.	8 30	9 35	1040	1245		4 40	6 25		7 30					
Barmouth........ mrn	7 10		9 10		c	1230	aft	2 42		3 50	Stop	4 40		6 0	7 35		10 0 5 0
Dyffryn	5 10		Stop		9 17		1240	2 15	2 52					6 10	7 45		5 10
Llanbedr and Pen	5 20				9 26		1246	2 25	2 58		b			6 16	7 53		5 18
Harlech ... [sarn	5 30				9 36		1256	2 35	3 8		b			6 33	8 11		5 29
Talsarnau	5 40				9 43		1 3	2 43	3 15					6 38	8 16		5 37
Penrhyndudraeth			mrn	9 48		1 7	2 49	3 19					6 44	8 22		5 42
Minffordd 351	5 50		mrn	9 51		1 13	2 55	3 27					6 48	8 26		5 49
Portmadoc §	5 55	5 30	6 55	9 55	9 59		1 17	3 0	3 32		5 18		6 53	8 31		5 52
Criccieth		5 37	8		1017		1 34		3 50		aft	5 32		7 10	8 47	aft	5 59
Afon Wen 361	6 07	15 10	5	1025		1 41			4 55			7 15	8 55	9 40	6 13
361 CARNARVON arr	8 21	1050	1145		2 55		5 19				1027	1027		7 52
Abererch	Sig.	Sig.	Sig.	Sig.		Sig.		Sig.		Sig.			Sig.	Sig.	Sig.		Sig. Sig.
Pwllheli ....arr.	6 10	7 30	1020	1050		2 0		4 20		5 55	45		7 25	9 10	9 50		8 58 6 25

* Station for Llanfair; † for Devil's Bridge; ‡ for Cader Idris; § for Beddgelert.
‖ ¼ mile to the Tal-y-llyn Company's Station.

a Stops for 1st class Passengers from or to local Stations, and 1,2,3, class from or to Stations on other Companies' Lines, notice to be given to Guard to set down. b Stop by signal to take up or set down Passengers booked from or to other Companies' Lines, notice to be given to Guard to set down. c Arrives at 11 50 mrn. d Except Sunday nights. e Stops by signal to take up for beyond Moat Lane. f Stops to set down from beyond Welshpool on informing Guard, and by signal to take up for Borth and Aberystwyth.
fl Stops to set down on informing Guard. g Stop to set down from beyond Machynlleth.
h Stop to take up for Newtown. k Stops to set down from beyond Shrewsbury or Crewe. 1 Saturday night.
j Stop to take up or set down to or from Stations beyond Birmingham, Hereford, and beyond. K Stops to set down from beyond Machynlleth.
Stops on Tuesdays to set down from Newtown.
Stops to take up for Birmingham, Hereford, and beyond. k Stops to set down from beyond Machynlleth. g Stop to set down on informing Guard, and by signal to take up for beyond Machynlleth. ✠ Stop to set down on informing Guard.
Runs 55 minutes earlier on the last Tuesday in the month.

1. Oswestry to Whitchurch
OSWESTRY

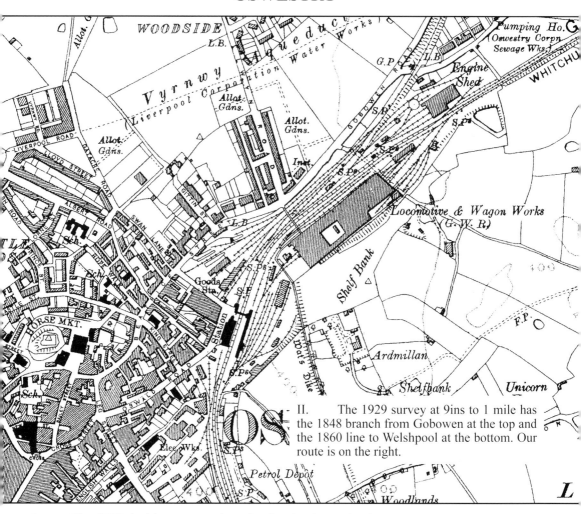

II.   The 1929 survey at 9ins to 1 mile has the 1848 branch from Gobowen at the top and the 1860 line to Welshpool at the bottom. Our route is on the right.

1.   The GWR had its own terminus for the shuttle service from Gobowen and it is seen in 1928, in use as a parcels shed. It had replaced an earlier structure in about 1885 and was not used by passengers after 1924, when a bay platform was added to the main station. (C.C.Green)

2.   The map shows a long footbridge northwest of the works; this picture was taken from it on 6th August 1935. From left to right are the 6-ton capacity crane, the Gobowen line running into the distance, North Box (96-levers), the Whitchurch line, the engine shed and the works. Centre is 517 class 0-4-2T no. 848 arriving with an autocoach from Gobowen. The two coaches on the right generally ran to Llanfyllin. (H.F.Wheeller/R.S.Carpenter coll.)

3.　　Outside the engine shed on 7th June 1936 is "Dean Goods" 0-6-0 no. 2401. The GWR shed code OSW was used at that time. There were 36 locomotives here in 1947 and later the shed was re-roofed. (A.N.H.Glover/F.A.Wycherley)

4.　　Victorian elegance is seen at its best on 18th June 1949. "Duke" class 4-4-0 no. 9087 *Mercury* waits with the 2.5pm from Whitchurch and behind it is the former head office of the CR. The train should arrive at Aberystwyth at 6.0pm. (P.W.Gray)

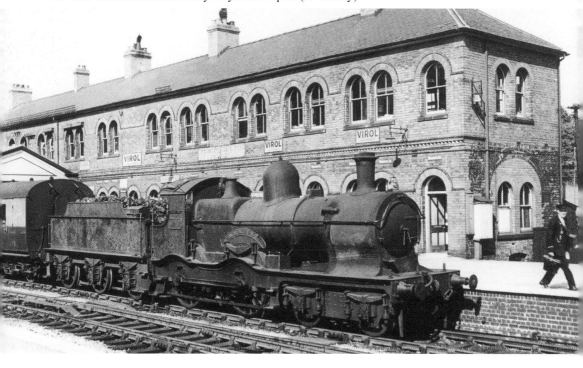

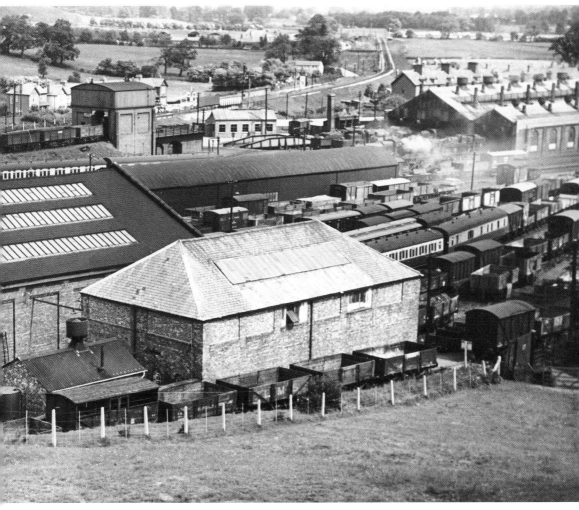

5.   On the right of this northward view from 31st May 1953 is the engine shed, with its new roof, plus the single line to Gobowen. Left of centre is the water tank, which is over the coal stage, and also visible is the turntable. The nearer buildings form the works. Its west end acted as the carriage shed. (R.Mulford)

Photographs of the north-south route and a more detailed map can be found in our *Branch Lines around Oswestry*.

6.   It is 30th June 1956 and 0-6-0PT no. 5401 waits in the 1924 bay with a train for Gobowen. South Box is in the distance; it had 42 levers. Both signal boxes closed on 8th November 1970. (H.C.Casserley)

7.   Only two of the four coaches of this Gobowen train are in use in this later view. The former GWR terminus can be seen above the nearest two coaches. The branch passenger service was withdrawn on 7th November 1966. (R.S.Carpenter)

8.   The 1.35pm to Whitchurch was hauled by 0-6-0 no. 5330 on 27th October 1962. With trains often standing at the platforms for long periods, the through line was useful for goods traffic. (E.Wilmshurst)

9.   The well ventilated shed is seen from a vantage point close to the works in November 1964; hence the low lighting and frost. The final BR code was 6E and closure came on 18th January 1965. (A.M.Davies)

10.   Recorded in October 1964 were 2-6-0 no. 46516 and 2-6-4T no. 80131. The CR goods yard had been to the left of the camera and it was this area which was leased (in part) by the Cambrian Railways Society in 1972. By 2010, the Cambrian Heritage Railway had been formed and was carrying passengers on this site and also at Llynclys. Shropshire County Council had acquired the route between Gobowen and Blodwell; thus a long journey had become a possibility. (A.M.Davies)

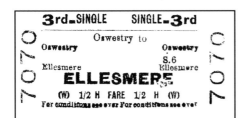

11.   This panorama is from the works footbridge on 3rd March 1967. The goods yard was in use until 6th December 1971. Stone trains from Llanddu Quarry continued to pass by until 28th October 1989. (E.Wilmshurst)

12.   The west elevation was recorded shortly after removal of the sign over the entrance. It can be seen in picture 14. The CR had applied the term "General Offices" to these premises. The upper storey housed the Cambrian directors' boardroom. (Colour-Rail.com)

13.   Part of the coal stack had presumably been used earlier as missiles on lower window targets. The main building survived vandals, official and otherwise. (G.Cryer/R.Mulford)

14.   The CRS established its splendid museum in the only surviving O&NR goods shed. It was used by the CR throughout its existence and was photographed in March 2000. Ten years later, the prospects were improving for the operation of tourist trains on the nearby disused mineral line. (M.Turvey)

TINKERS GREEN HALT

15.   A westward view from 1958 shows that electric light had arrived. The halt opened on 16th October 1939, in the dark days of the war, when blackout prevailed. The halt served the Army camp at Park Hall. (Stations UK)

16.   Looking in the other direction in April 1962, we see part of the camp. Park Hall had also been used for military purposes in World War I and a halt was provided on the branch from Gobowen to Oswestry. (J.Langford)

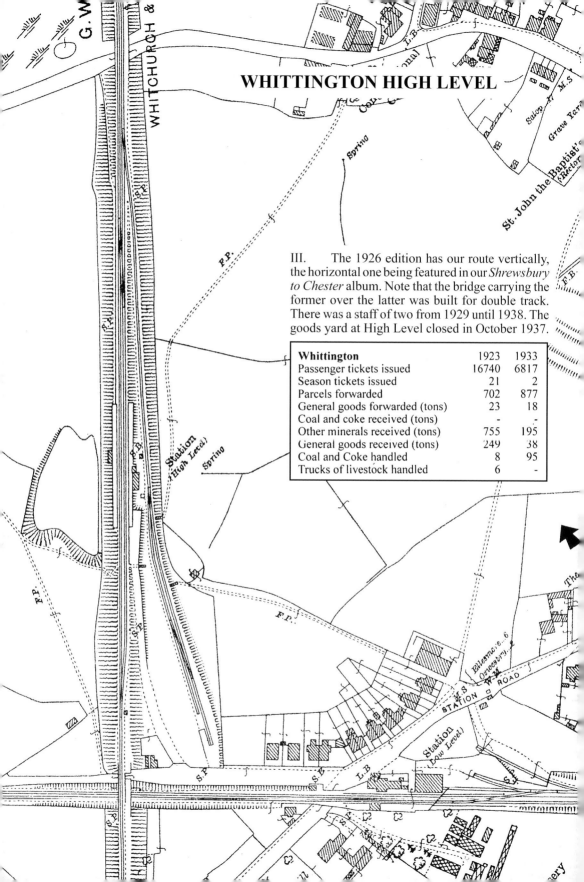

WHITTINGTON HIGH LEVEL

III.   The 1926 edition has our route vertically, the horizontal one being featured in our *Shrewsbury to Chester* album. Note that the bridge carrying the former over the latter was built for double track. There was a staff of two from 1929 until 1938. The goods yard at High Level closed in October 1937.

Whittington	1923	1933
Passenger tickets issued	16740	6817
Season tickets issued	21	2
Parcels forwarded	702	877
General goods forwarded (tons)	23	18
Coal and coke received (tons)	-	-
Other minerals received (tons)	755	195
General goods received (tons)	249	38
Coal and Coke handled	8	95
Trucks of livestock handled	6	-

17.   A 1935 view north reveals that all the buildings and also the platforms were made of timber; this minimised the weight on the embankment. Near the pole on the right is the small signal box. It had 19 levers and was in use from July 1899 until January 1960. (Stations UK)

18.   This closer view of the box is from 29th July 1959. The suffix was added on 1st July 1924 and the station closed to passengers earlier than the others on the route, on 4th January 1960. Low Level closed on 12th September of that year. (E.Wilmshurst)

FRANKTON HALT

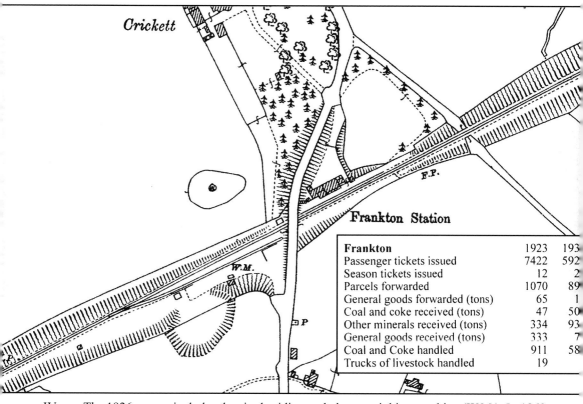

Crickett

F.P.

Frankton Station

Frankton	1923	193
Passenger tickets issued	7422	592
Season tickets issued	12	2
Parcels forwarded	1070	89
General goods forwarded (tons)	65	1
Coal and coke received (tons)	47	50
Other minerals received (tons)	334	93
General goods received (tons)	333	7
Coal and Coke handled	911	58
Trucks of livestock handled	19	

IV.   The 1926 survey includes the single siding and also a weighing machine (W.M.). In 1869, there were just two trains to Oswestry and three called by request in the other direction. There was an eight lever signal box until 1929.

19.   The station opened later than the others, sometime in January 1867. Fascinating features are the fine finials and the company's crest in moulded terracotta . There were two men here until 1934 and just one thereafter. (Lens of Sutton coll.)

20.   The station was downgraded to a halt on 13th June 1955 and staffing ceased on 1st March 1956. The photograph is from 1958. (Stations UK)

21.   The date is 5th October 1962 and no. 7809 *Childrey Manor* is passing the goods yard, which was closed on 6th July 1964, but was clearly little used long before then. The train is the 1.50pm from Oswestry to Crewe. (R.G.Nelson/T.Walsh)

22.   The neglected site was recorded on 29th March 1965, but the locomotive details were not. At least the allotment was well cared for. (P.Ward/SLS)

23.   The impressive north elevation was photographed on July 1965. The upper and lower window styles are replicated on the other side. The terracotta CR crest was repeated in the other two gable elevations. (M.Lloyd/WRRC)

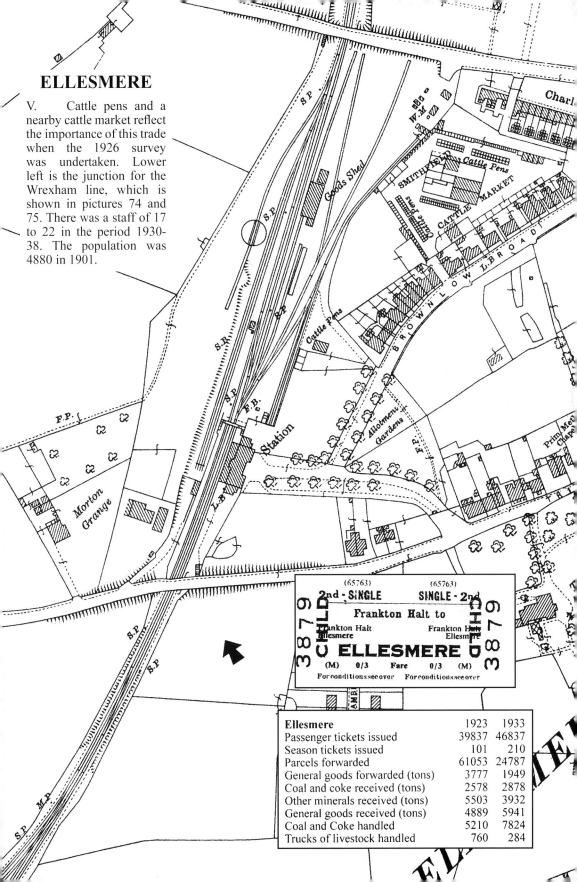

ELLESMERE

V.   Cattle pens and a nearby cattle market reflect the importance of this trade when the 1926 survey was undertaken. Lower left is the junction for the Wrexham line, which is shown in pictures 74 and 75. There was a staff of 17 to 22 in the period 1930-38. The population was 4880 in 1901.

Frankton Halt to
ELLESMERE

Ellesmere	1923	1933
Passenger tickets issued	39837	46837
Season tickets issued	101	210
Parcels forwarded	61053	24787
General goods forwarded (tons)	3777	1949
Coal and coke received (tons)	2578	2878
Other minerals received (tons)	5503	3932
General goods received (tons)	4889	5941
Coal and Coke handled	5210	7824
Trucks of livestock handled	760	284

24.   Our earliest picture is an eastward view from the main road and it shows a building style employed elsewhere by the CR, Llanidloes being similar. (J.M.Strange/S.C.Jenkins coll.)

25.   A 1923 photograph reveals that milk was another important local traffic. By the early 1930s, most was conveyed by tanker and this form of platform ornamentation ceased. (Stations UK)

26. We look west from the northern bridge in 1947, with the goods yard on the left and the turntable siding to the right of the ringed shunt signals. The table was 50ft in length. (Stations UK)

27. A Whitchurch to Oswestry train arrives on 22nd June 1956, hauled by 4-4-0 no. 9021, one of a type introduced in 1936. A crane of 6-ton capacity was listed in 1938. (Lens of Sutton coll.)

28.   The Wrexham push-pull train is using the crossover on 30th June 1956, prior to departure in front of 0-4-2T no. 1432. The coach was only two years old at that time. (H.C.Casserley)

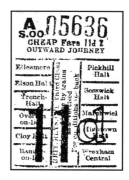

29.   A panorama from 21st June 1959 allows study of the west elevation and the remarkable window styling. The immaculate gardens are particularly noteworthy. (P.J.Garland/R.S.Carpenter)

30.   The building accommodated the offices of the OE&WR initially and subsequently those of the W&ER. Sadly, the structure became neglected in its later years, but it has been restored for commercial use. (C.C.Green/S.C.Jenkins coll.)

31.   We can now enjoy three photographs from 19th May 1962. Here we see 4-6-0 no. 7807 *Compton Manor* arriving from Oswestry. (P.J.Garland/R.S.Carpenter)

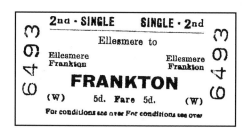

32.   A close up of the running-in board helps to explain why no litter is visible in any photograph. However, they do not show any signal finials to be missing. (P.J.Garland/R.S.Carpenter)

33.   Destined for Whitchurch is no. 7807 (seen in picture 31) and waiting to propel its coach to Wrexham is 0-4-2T no. 1458. This service would cease within four months. There was a 32-lever signal box. (P.J.Garland/R.S.Carpenter)

34. The nameboard was stark after 1962 and vegetation went largely unchecked. The station was lit by gas to the end. Southbound is class 2 2-6-2T no. 41241, a type introduced in 1946. (Dr. G.B.Sutton)

35. There were only a few days of working left when this photograph was taken in the frost of early January 1965. The wagons were probably empty ones being stored. Goods traffic ceased on 29th March 1965. (A.M.Davies)

WELSHAMPTON

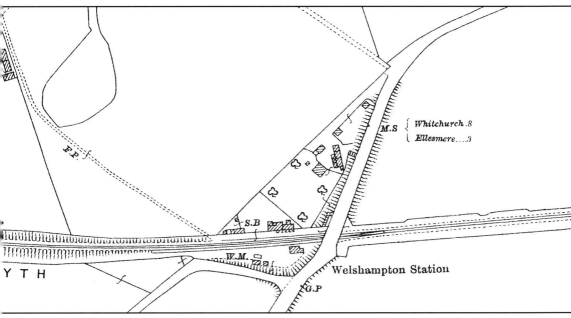

VI.   A single short siding can be found on the south side of the line on this 1926 extract. There were 489 souls resident in 1901 and 388 in 1961. The signal box lasted until 1929. It had nine levers and was not a block post.

36.   A postcard from around 1910 shows a CR economy measure in goods shed provision. A retired coach has been fitted with a sliding door and an extended roof. It seems that coal came from Staffordshire, rather than the nearby collieries. (Lens of Sutton coll.)

37.   The parcels shed is seen more clearly in this later record, which includes traditional oil lamps and a sign announcing: YOU MAY TELEPHONE FROM HERE. The location was the scene of a dreadful accident in June 1897, when a returning Sunday School excursion from Barmouth to Royton in Lancashire left the rails. In the ensuing pile-up, nine children were killed and 16 seriously injured. (Stations UK)

Welshampton	1923	1933
Passenger tickets issued	5229	4272
Season tickets issued	5	23
Parcels forwarded	1079	818
General goods forwarded (tons)	36	21
Coal and coke received (tons)	23	33
Other minerals received (tons)	174	786
General goods received (tons)	734	163
Coal and Coke handled	1049	507
Trucks of livestock handled	-	-

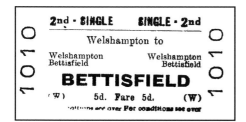

38.   Business was relatively brisk on 19th May 1962 as a period fashion show took place by assorted figures. Traffic figures were similarly variable by that time. (P.J.Garland/R.S.Carpenter)

39.   The nameboard was in terminal decline and no explanation has been found for Welshampton being in England. (P.J.Garland/R.S.Carpenter)

40.   The survey was completed that day as the train departed and tickets were collected. The churn was for fresh water for the staff. One man was listed here in the 1929-38 period. (P.J.Garland/R.S.Carpenter)

41.   An eastward view from the 1960s shows the inevitable decline; the sheds and lamps have vanished and a lone couple wait for the approaching train. Goods traffic ceased on 4th May 1964. (W.A.Camwell/SLS)

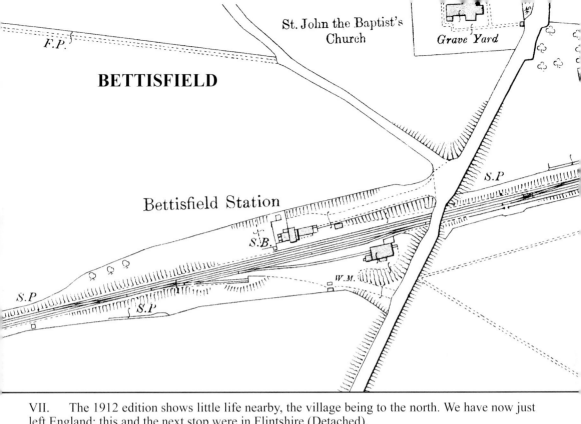

BETTISFIELD

St. John the Baptist's Church

Grave Yard

F.P.

Bettisfield Station

S.P.

S.B.

W.M.

S.P.

S.P.

VII.   The 1912 edition shows little life nearby, the village being to the north. We have now just left England; this and the next stop were in Flintshire (Detached).

42.   The passenger's perspective was photographed on 30th June 1956. At night, the name was illuminated by the wick of an oil lamp. (H.C.Casserley)

43.   Three men were in attendance in the 1930s, but they did not unload coal. This was the merchants' task. This blurred view is from 1954. (Stations UK)

44.   The east end of the loop was recorded in October 1960, with CR and GWR posts evident. The signalling allowed both lines to be used in both directions. (R.G.Nelson/T.Walsh)

45.   Heating steam issues from the rear of a westbound train in February 1962. The 4-6-0 is no. 7820 *Dinmore Manor* and it is now preserved on the West Somerset Railway. It was built in 1950. (J.W.T.House/C.L.Caddy coll.)

Bettisfield	1923	1933
Passenger tickets issued	7326	4857
Season tickets issued	35	14
Parcels forwarded	2692	1460
General goods forwarded (tons)	204	43
Coal and coke received (tons)	115	318
Other minerals received (tons)	384	147
General goods received (tons)	1024	361
Coal and Coke handled	1773	1360
Trucks of livestock handled	73	18

46.   An April 1962 view from the other side of the road bridge reveals that the goods yard could be served by trains running in either direction. The signal box was in use from 2nd October 1926 to 18th January 1965 and it housed 36 levers. (B.W.L.Brooksbank)

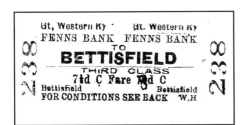

47.   It is 19th May 1962 and 4-6-0 no. 7803 *Barcote Manor* runs in with a Welshpool to Whitchurch train. The hoop carried a single line tablet and the porter/signalman will not gain wet trousers when he mounts his own transport, seen beyond him. (P.J.Garland/R.S.Carpenter)

48.   No. 46511 is a 2-6-0 with an eastbound freight train, standing close to the staff transport. Being a dry day, it is parked in the open. To the left of it is the cattle dock. (A.M.Davies)

49.   Minutes later and we depart west to gain a panoramic view of the station. The goods yard closed on 4th May 1964. (A.M.Davics)

50.   Both the goods shed and the main building had become dwellings. They were photographed in June 2009, along with Baguley Drewry no. 2107, which had been on show near Oswestry Works until July 2008. (B.Dotson)

FENNS BANK

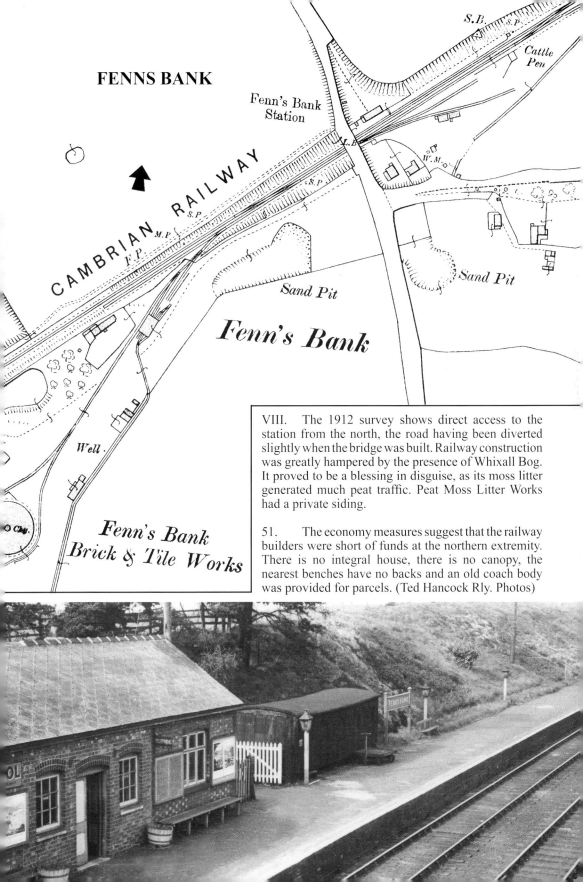

FENN'S BANK

Fenn's Bank Station

CAMBRIAN RAILWAY

Fenn's Bank

Sand Pit

Sand Pit

Cattle Pen

S.B.

W.M.

L.B.

S.P.

S.P.

F.P.

M.P.

Well

Fenn's Bank
Brick & Tile Works

VIII. The 1912 survey shows direct access to the station from the north, the road having been diverted slightly when the bridge was built. Railway construction was greatly hampered by the presence of Whixall Bog. It proved to be a blessing in disguise, as its moss litter generated much peat traffic. Peat Moss Litter Works had a private siding.

51. The economy measures suggest that the railway builders were short of funds at the northern extremity. There is no integral house, there is no canopy, the nearest benches have no backs and an old coach body was provided for parcels. (Ted Hancock Rly. Photos)

52.   Looking northeast in February 1963, we see stock standing in the long refuge siding and a train signalled from Whitchurch. The signal box was in use from 1st September 1890 until 18th January 1965. (A.M.Davies)

Fenn's Bank	1923	1933
Passenger tickets issued	6407	3307
Season tickets issued	6	20
Parcels forwarded	1853	2781
General goods forwarded (tons)	316	365
Coal and coke received (tons)	106	198
Other minerals received (tons)	2149	405
General goods received (tons)	2642	351
Coal and Coke handled	3494	4825
Trucks of livestock handled	50	14

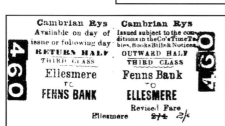

53.   The north end of the siding is seen in January 1965. It is apparent that the earthworks were constructed to allow for double track. The goods yard closed on 5th April 1964. (A.M.Davies)

54.   The simple facilities were supplemented by a small lamp room, left. There were three men employed here in the 1930s. The building and the weigh house are still intact. (W.A.Camwell/SLS)

SOUTH OF WHITCHURCH

55.   We are back in England and looking south from the former LNWR main line to Shrewsbury, from the 9.45am Whitchurch to Aberystwyth on 16th January 1965, the last day of operation. The CR began on the curve. (A.M.Davies)

WHITCHURCH (SALOP)

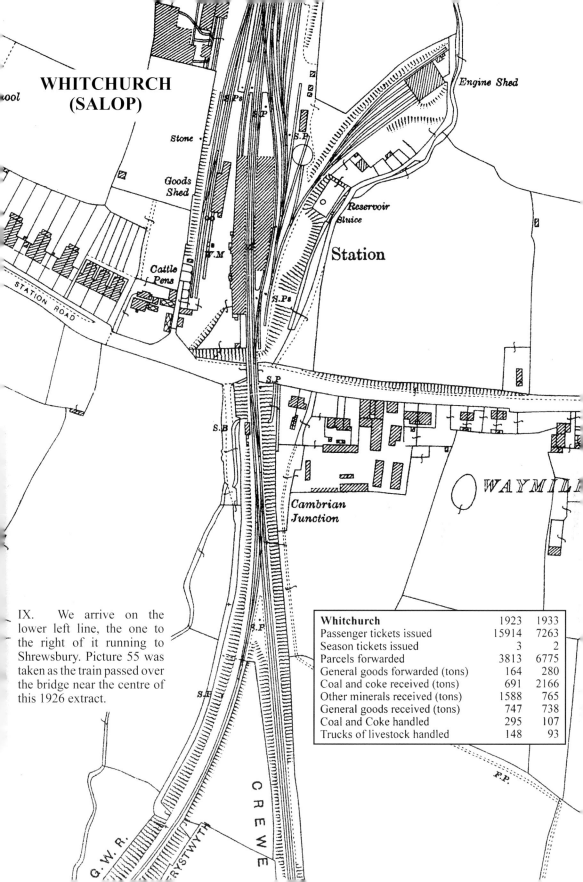

Stone

Goods Shed

Cattle Pens

STATION ROAD

S.P.

S.P.

S.P.

W.M

S.Ps

S.P.

S.B

Engine Shed

Reservoir Sluice

Station

S.P.

S.P.

S.B

Cambrian Junction

WAYMILL

S.B

Q. W. R.

CREWE

ABERYSTWYTH

F.P.

IX. We arrive on the lower left line, the one to the right of it running to Shrewsbury. Picture 55 was taken as the train passed over the bridge near the centre of this 1926 extract.

Whitchurch	1923	1933
Passenger tickets issued	15914	7263
Season tickets issued	3	2
Parcels forwarded	3813	6775
General goods forwarded (tons)	164	280
Coal and coke received (tons)	691	2166
Other minerals received (tons)	1588	765
General goods received (tons)	747	738
Coal and Coke handled	295	107
Trucks of livestock handled	148	93

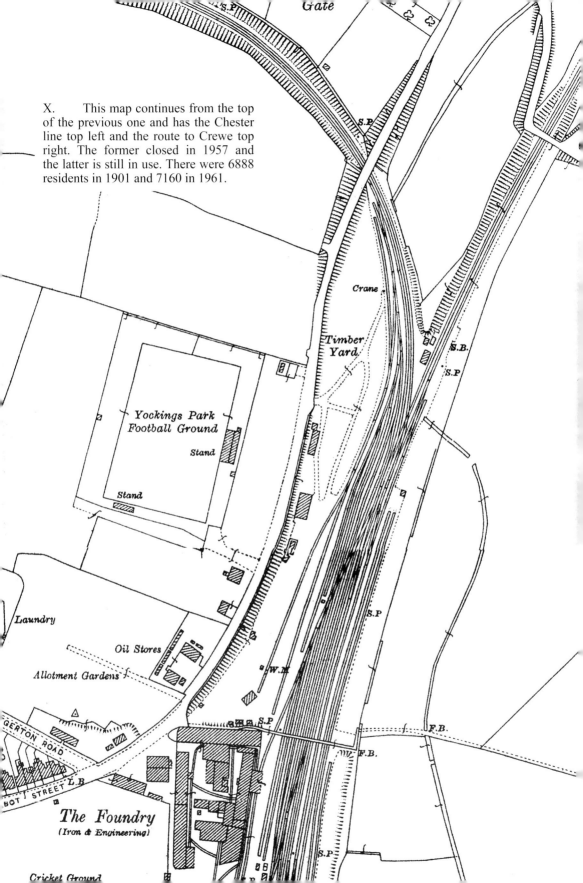

X.   This map continues from the top of the previous one and has the Chester line top left and the route to Crewe top right. The former closed in 1957 and the latter is still in use. There were 6888 residents in 1901 and 7160 in 1961.

Gate

S.P

S.B.

Crane

Timber Yard

S.B.

S.P

Yockings Park Football Ground

Stand

Stand

Laundry

Oil Stores

S.P

Allotment Gardens

W.M

GERTON ROAD

F.B.

S.P

F.B.

F.B.

L.B

BOT STREET

The Foundry
(Iron & Engineering)

S.P

Cricket Ground

56.   A view from about 1923 is of the island platform, which was designated up (to London) by the LNWR and its successors. On the empty milk churns is a pigeon basket. Such racing brought vast revenue to the railways. (Stations UK)

57.	A 1949 panorama includes the bay platform, which was at the north end and was often used by Chester trains. Cambrian Junction box is in the distance. (Stations UK)

58.	Seen on 10th September 1951 is an Oswestry train hauled by 0-6-0 no. 2409, a "Dean Goods". The class was introduced in 1883. (R.M.Casserley coll.)

59.　　Looking north, we have the bay platform and the goods yard on the left. Suggs Rochester pattern gas lamps are also included. Freight traffic ceased on 1st October 1976. (Lens of Sutton coll.)

60.　　A panorama from the footbridge includes the water tank, turntable and engine shed. The rotten roof supports are evident. (Lens of Sutton coll.)

61. At the north end on 27th August 1954 is (left) 2-6-0 no. 46514 having arrived with the 4.35pm from Llanfyllin. On the right, class 2P 4-4-0 no. 40589 waits with the 6.45pm to Chester. (H.C.Casserley)

62.　　　Outside the shed on 27th August 1954 was class 4 4-6-0 no. 75023. The shed was not used regularly after 1957, except for locomotives on trial from Crewe Works. (R.M.Casserley)

63.　　　The turntable was 60ft long and was carrying 2-6-0 no. 46510 when photographed on 28th June 1958. Sweat and toil went with grease and oil. (G.Adams/M.J.Stretton coll.)

64.   A wander along the down platform on the same day would bring the joys of gazing at simmering giants and also reciting the principal stations of the former CR. (G.Adams/M.J.Stretton coll.)

65.   Seen from the south end of the down platform on 5th October 1960 is a train of milk tanks, hauled by 0-6-0 no. 2233, one of the 2251 class. (R.G.Nelson/T.Walsh)

66.   We can enjoy all the trackwork east of the platforms in this photograph of no. 41241 waiting to leave for Oswestry. (Dr. G.B.Sutton)

67.   The same train is shown from a different angle which enables us to see the lines to the locomotive depot more fully. Under the ground on the right is a reservoir for engine water. (Dr. G.B.Sutton)

68.   The main building was unimposing when compared with the main CR structures. The bus shows: D87 OSWESTRY and HAMPSON. It is a 1951 AEC Regal IV, ex-London Transport class RF. (Stations UK)

69.   Seen from platform 4 sometime in 1962 is a train departing for Shrewsbury and beyond, while an ex-GWR locomotive waits to leave for the Oswestry line. The aerial ironwork also intrudes into picture 60. (Stations UK)

70.   Cambrian Junction box is in the distance in this southward view from 19th May 1962 and eight of its signals appear. (P.J.Garland/R.S.Carpenter)

71.   A closer look at the box fails to include milepost 0, which is where Cambrian measurements started (and still do so). The frame had 45 levers and closure of the box came in June 1969. (A.M.Davies)

72.   An Oswestry train is behind 0-6-0 no. 2271 as a DMU arrives from Crewe in 1964. The station would soon receive long overdue surgery. (A.M.Davies)

73.   We rush forward to 16th August 1984 to see the results and also the 09.20 Crewe to Shrewsbury DMU. Subsequently, two bus shelters have been deemed to be sufficient. (D.H.Mitchell)

2. Wrexham Branch
WEST OF ELLESMERE

74.   We look south from the road bridge below the centre of map V (after picture 23) and see the double track from the station merging and then dividing again: left to Oswestry and right to Wrexham. The year is 1959. (P.J.Garland/R.S.Carpenter)

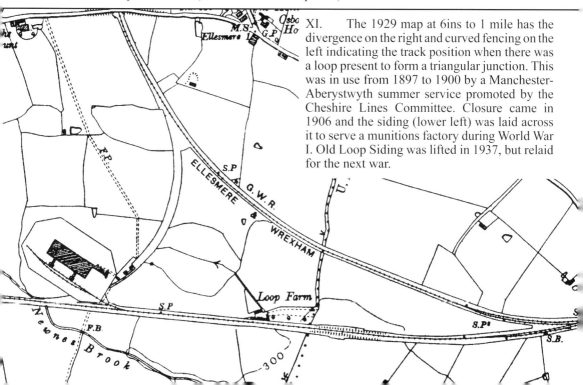

XI.   The 1929 map at 6ins to 1 mile has the divergence on the right and curved fencing on the left indicating the track position when there was a loop present to form a triangular junction. This was in use from 1897 to 1900 by a Manchester-Aberystwyth summer service promoted by the Cheshire Lines Committee. Closure came in 1906 and the siding (lower left) was laid across it to serve a munitions factory during World War I. Old Loop Siding was lifted in 1937, but relaid for the next war.

75.　　　Ellesmere North Junction was at the top of the triangle and its box was photographed in 1962. It once housed 24 levers. It was probably used by the permanent way gang, whose trolley hut is on the right. (P.J.Garland/R.S.Carpenter)

Branch Gradient Profile.

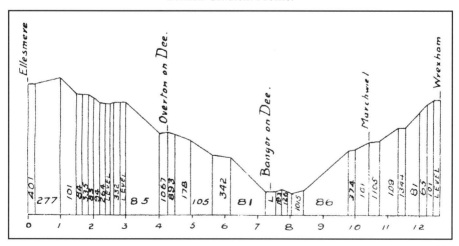

ELSON HALT

76.   A 1956 shot from the road bridge shows a train being propelled from Ellesmere. The halt had opened on 8th January 1937 and, like all other stops on the route, was closed for most of World War II. (A.M.Davies)

77.   The bridge carries the B5068 and, like the others on the branch, was built for double track. This is a view from a departing train on 30th June 1956. Elson siding was ¼ mile to the north, on the east side of the line. This closed in the 1930s, but was reinstated for wartime stores traffic. (H.C.Casserley)

TRENCH HALT

78.   The platform was brought into use in December 1914, to serve local villages. There was also a private siding in 1938-41. The photograph is from 1954 and we are looking towards Ellesmere. (Stations UK)

79.   Trench is in Wales, but its halt was in England. This 1956 picture shows the distance from Ellesmere and a post to carry an oil lamp. (H.C.Casserley)

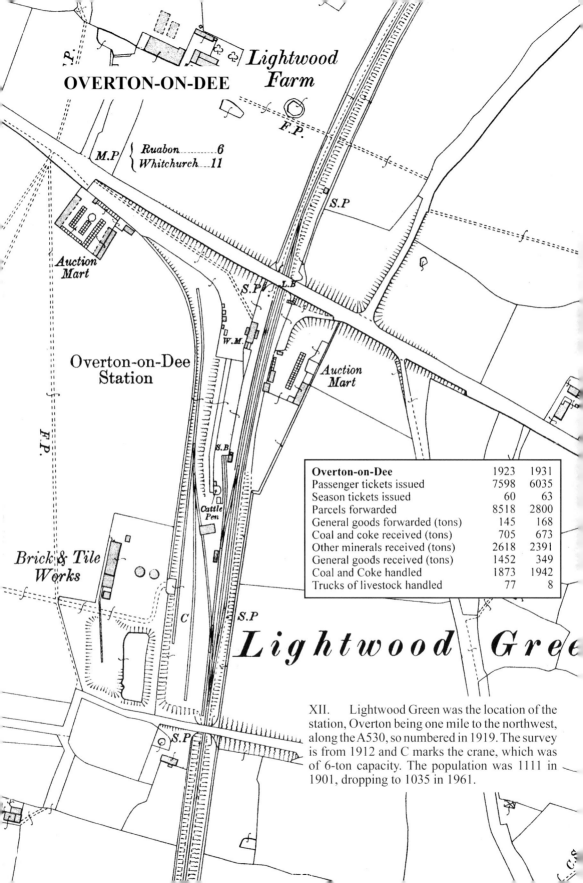

OVERTON-ON-DEE

Lightwood Farm

F.P.

M.P. { Ruabon..........6
Whitchurch....11 }

S.P

Auction Mart

S.P. L.B

W.M.

Overton-on-Dee Station

S.B

F.P.

Auction Mart

Cattle Pen

Brick & Tile Works

C   S.P

S.P.

Lightwood Gree

Overton-on-Dee	1923	1931
Passenger tickets issued	7598	6035
Season tickets issued	60	63
Parcels forwarded	8518	2800
General goods forwarded (tons)	145	168
Coal and coke received (tons)	705	673
Other minerals received (tons)	2618	2391
General goods received (tons)	1452	349
Coal and Coke handled	1873	1942
Trucks of livestock handled	77	8

XII.   Lightwood Green was the location of the station, Overton being one mile to the northwest, along the A530, so numbered in 1919. The survey is from 1912 and C marks the crane, which was of 6-ton capacity. The population was 1111 in 1901, dropping to 1035 in 1961.

80.   The staffing dropped from four in 1923 to two in 1932, as it did at the two stations to the north. The dairy is on the right; CWS stands for Co-operative Wholesale Society. In the centre background is the brickworks. (P.Ward/SLS coll.)

81.   There was a 10mph speed limit through the station. Class 4500 2-6-2T no. 4578 has arrived from Wrexham in 1958, with the junction in the background. This class was introduced in 1906. (H.F.Wheeller/R.S.Carpenter coll.)

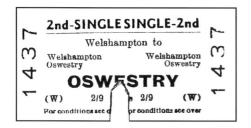

1437   2nd-SINGLE SINGLE-2nd   1437
Welshampton to
Welshampton   Welshampton
Oswestry   Oswestry
OSWESTRY
(W)   2/9   2/9   (W)
For conditions see o   or conditions see over

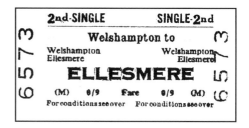

6573   2nd-SINGLE   SINGLE-2nd   3
Welshampton to
Welshampton   Welshampton
Ellesmere   Ellesmere
ELLESMERE   5
(M)   0/9   Fare   0/9   (M)   6
For conditions see over   For conditions see over

82.   The foot crossing is included in this panorama from May 1958, as is the northern limit of the long loop. Its southern end is in the next picture, taken on the same day. (H.F.Wheeller/R.S.Carpenter coll.)

83.   On the right is the connection to the goods yard. Its traffic ceased when passenger services were withdrawn on 10th September 1962. (H.F.Wheeller/R.S.Carpenter coll.)

84.   We move into the box on the same day to find the kettle on. The 24-lever frame had replaced one with 16 levers. (H.F.Wheeller/R.S.Carpenter coll.)

85.   A train for Wrexham arrives and passes a goods train, hauled by 0-6-0PT no. 3789. On the left is the cattle dock. (A.M.Davies)

86.   Weed growth was advanced only one week before closure. Total receipts dropped from £3549 in 1923 to £472 in 1932. (C.C.Green)

CLOY HALT

87.   Opened earlier as Caedyah Halt, but not in the timetables, this facility was provided from 1st July 1932. Sadly, the Pagoda shelters had long gone by then. This view towards Wrexham is from 30th June 1956. (H.C.Casserley)

BANGOR-ON-DEE

XIII.   The 1912 survey does not include Bangor, as it was ¾ mile west of the station. It once had a monastery and one of its monks founded another in northwest Wales, using the same name, without anticipating the problems it would cause in future railway timetables.

Bangor-on-Dee	1923	1931
Passenger tickets issued	11146	8546
Season tickets issued	65	70
Parcels forwarded	11973	1562
General goods forwarded (tons)	371	204
Coal and coke received (tons)	679	465
Other minerals received (tons)	4008	916
General goods received (tons)	1224	284
Coal and Coke handled	2723	679
Trucks of livestock handled	208	58

88.   A white lamp with clear glass indicates the front end of the train in this 1954 view. The posters offer many attractive destinations. There were 528 residents in 1961. (Stations UK)

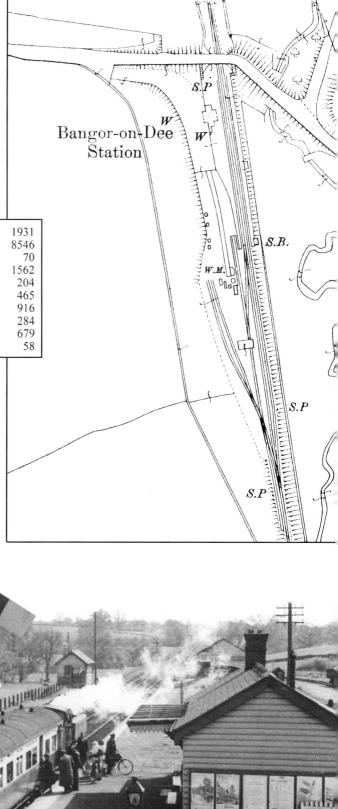

89.   The goods shed differed from the one at Overton and there was no crane. The goods train
has a 2-6-2T at its head and a "Toad" brake van at its tail. (P. Ward/SLS coll.)

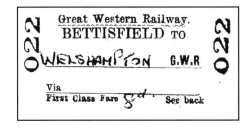

Great Western Railway.
BETTISFIELD TO
WELSHAMPTON G.W.R

Via
First Class Fare 5ᵈ   See back

022   022

90.   Storm clouds gather as 0-4-2T no. 1458 waits to proceed, but again the date is unknown. There was a signal box with 24 levers, contrasting with only 16 until 1919. (W.A.Camwell/SLS coll.)

91.   The loop here was even longer than the one at Overton, measuring 804ft. It had the same 10mph limit. (C.Gammell)

92. Both platforms had steps direct to the road and so no footbridge was provided. Seen in 1962 is an original CR tapered wooden signal post. (P.J.Garland/R.S.Carpenter)

93. No. 1458 is seen again with a train for Ellesmere. The date is 26th May 1962 and the staff seem to have lost the will to weed. (A.M.Davies)

94.   The bridge over the River Dee was about ¼ mile north of the station. No. 1432 is approaching it in June 1958. (A.M.Davies)

95.   The bowstring spans are seen from an autocoach on 30th June 1956. Their length was 66yds and the lattice girder construction was undertaken in Warrington. (H.C.Casserley)

PICKHILL HALT

96.   The halt opened on 30th May 1938 and was intended to serve Cadbury's creamery, the chimney of which is on the right. The siding did likewise and curves south in the distance. Five vans of chocolates left on most days; coal was the inward traffic. (C.C.Green)

97.   Moving onto the bridge, we can observe the Cadbury Works, on 9th September 1962. What is not evident is that the running line is on a gradient of 1 in 86, which meant that shunting had to be undertaken with great caution. (C.C.Green)

SESSWICK HALT

98.   This was an earlier halt, it opening in October 1913. It was busy in 1940, being used by workers building the Royal Ordnance Factory nearby. The platform is south of the B5130 and is seen in the 1960s. (Lens of Sutton coll.)

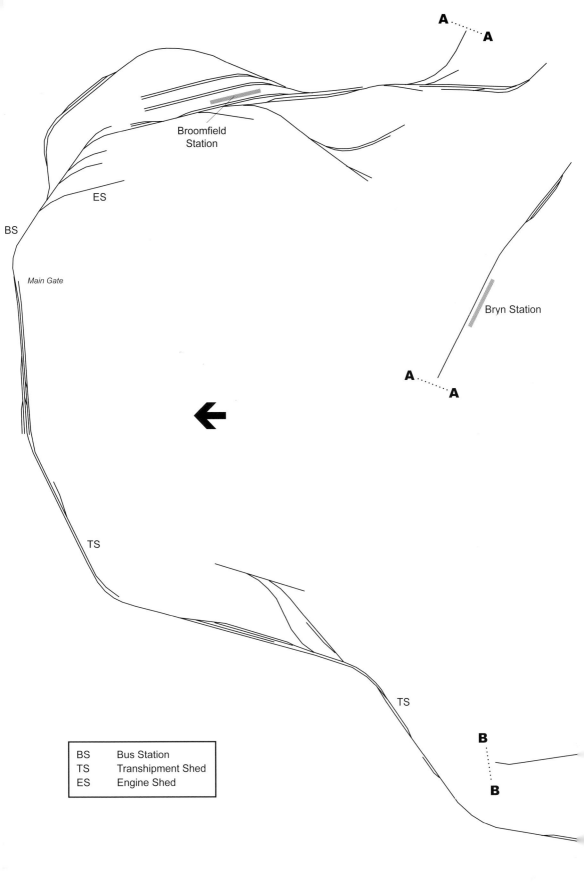

A········A

Broomfield
Station

ES

BS

Main Gate

Bryn Station

A········A

TS

TS

B
:
B

BS	Bus Station
TS	Transhipment Shed
ES	Engine Shed

EAST OF MARCHWIEL

One mile before reaching Marchwiel, a line branched off on the north side of the route to serve the Royal Ordnance Factory. As mentioned in caption 98, this was built soon after hostilities commenced and it generated a vast amount of rail traffic. A 1200ft long loop was provided, together with a 72-lever signal box. By 1943, there were four reception sidings and four for despatch, plus one for the works shunters. There was no narrow gauge system. The private siding agreement ended on 17th July 1961, but the siding was subsequently used by the Wrexham Trading Estate until 8th December 1971. The area is now known as the Wrexham Industrial Estate. This diagram is based on badly damaged official documents. The signal box on the GWR closed in May 1946. The stations had a service to and from Wrexham for workers, which numbered over 13,000 at their peak. In 1953, the North Western Gas Board opened a gas works, which used coal. In about 1960, alterations brought an oil plant, together with a regional stores depot and grid control room for North Wales. The gasworks had a siding, but it closed in about 1971, when a pipeline came into use.

Parkey Station

Five Ford
Station

TS

GWR

B

B

MARCHWIEL

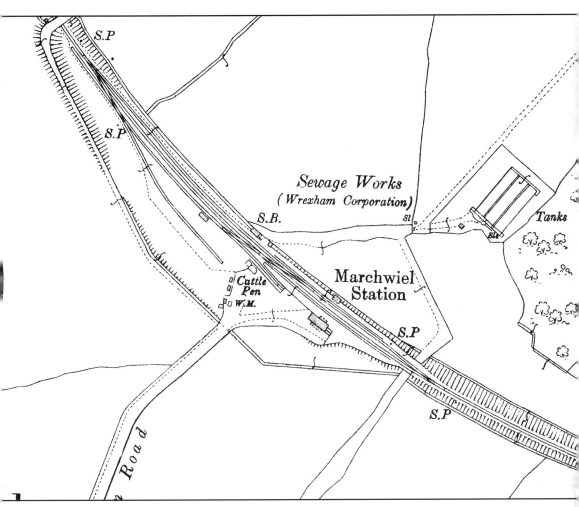

XIV.   The 1912 survey shows little of interest nearby, unless one is a sanitary student. Five Fords private siding was shown on the north side of the line ¼ mile to the east. It was in use in 1904-55, mainly for local farm produce.

Marchwiel	1923	1931
Passenger tickets issued	5733	5710
Season tickets issued	13	14
Parcels forwarded	12371	540
General goods forwarded (tons)	704	644
Coal and coke received (tons)	19	-
Other minerals received (tons)	4022	147
General goods received (tons)	813	591
Coal and Coke handled	1587	254
Trucks of livestock handled	177	24

99.   All the buildings were timber framed, timber clad and set back from the platform edge. There was also a signal box, with 30 levers, which was open until 7th June 1964. (W.A.Camwell/SLS coll.)

100.   It is 1st October 1955 and the 2.40pm Ellesmere to Wrexham is awaiting departure. The globe of the oil lamp is visible within the lantern. (W.A.Camwell/SLS coll.)

101.   A train is departing for Wrexham and we have a rare opportunity to examine the details of a loading gauge. The curved extremities remained raised except for load checking; this was to avoid decapitating members of footplate staff. (W.A.Camwell/SLS coll.)

102.   The goods yard is in the background, but it had no crane. The photograph is from June 1956 and it shows that the pleasant countryside was well wooded. (H.C.Casserley)

103.   A train for Ellesmere waits on 26th May 1962 behind 0-4-2T no. 1458. The goods yard (left) remained open until 4th September 1972, over a decade after the others on the branch. (A.M.Davies)

HIGHTOWN HALT

104.   The halt came into use on 9th July 1923 and a siding opened in 1941. It was a private one, ¼ mile to the south and served an aircraft components factory. It was used by Rubery Owens for their engineering works from 20th December 1947. The photograph is from 1956, in rain, looking south from Whitegate Road. (A.M.Davies)

EAST OF WREXHAM

XV.   The 1915 edition at 6ins to 1 mile has our route lower right. There was a MOD siding at Abenbury until 4th September 1972. There are two earlier sidings shown here, to brickworks. Kings Mill Viaduct is marked, as are embankments west of it. These never carried track, but were built in the 1860s as part of a line that would pass south of the urban area of Wrexham and link with the line north to Connah's Quay (later GCR). On entering the built-up area, our route passes the goods depot at Caia Road. Wrexham Central is at the join of the pages and the line continues round the curve to Wrexham General. This station and the straight main line are included in our *Shrewsbury to Chester* album.

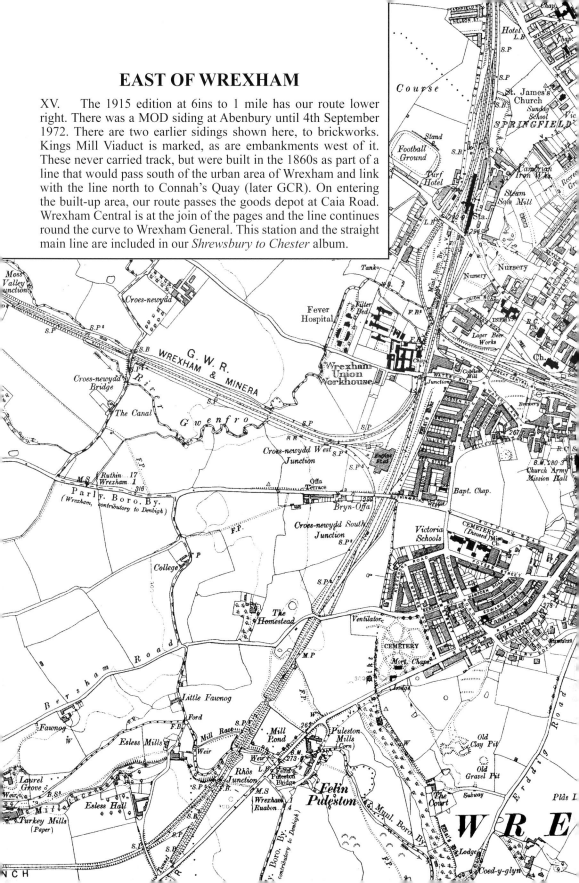

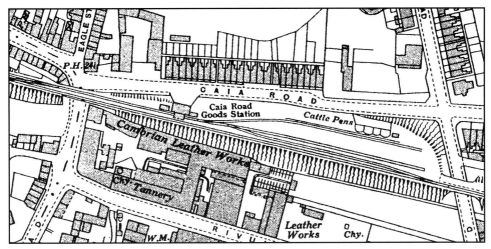

XVI. The extent of the yard at Caia Road is shown on the 1937 edition. The goods shed contained a 30cwt crane, but all traffic ceased on 2nd November 1964.

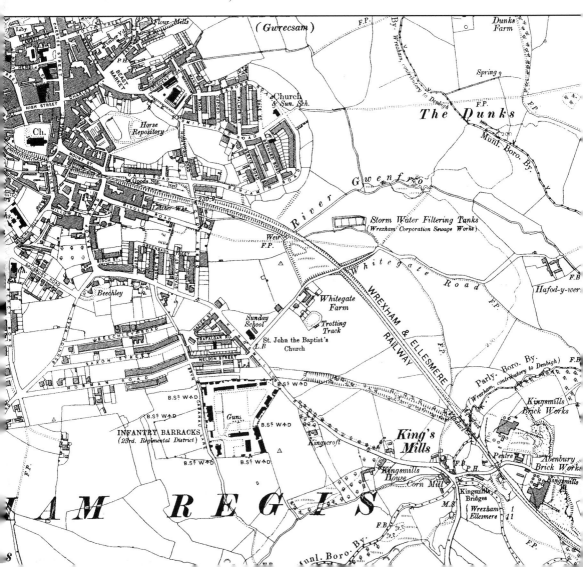

105. Kings Mill Viaduct was 84yds in length, but difficult to photograph in its entirety. Note that the abutments were built for double track. (C.C.Green)

106. Caia Goods Yard was photographed on 8th September 1962, with scrap metal being loaded in the background. The line under the roof was part of a loop, which continued east as a single line to Wrexham Central. (C.C.Green)

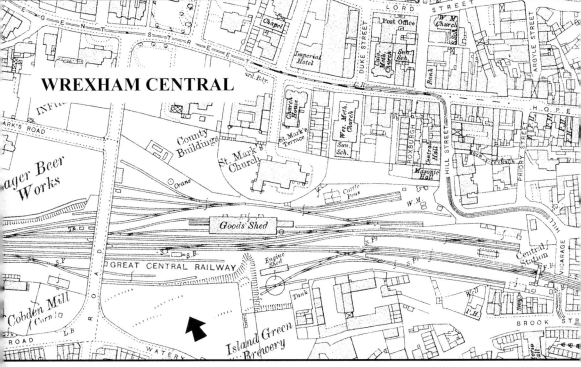

WREXHAM CENTRAL

XVII. The street tramway shown on this 1911 extract had horse trams from 1st November 1876 to 26th April 1901. Electric tramways operated from 4th April 1903 to 31st March 1927. Track gauge for both was 3ft 6ins. Churches of three denominations flanked the railway and two breweries are within a sniff of it. The turntable is close to the CR engine shed, which was moved to Aberayon in 1926. The table was 50ft in length.

107.   There were only two GWR employees here in the 1923-38 period, both signalmen. Others worked for the LNER. St. Giles Church is in the background and the Ellesmere train on the right will soon pass it. On the left are two bay platforms, which formed part of the 1887 terminus of the WM&CQR. The GCR took it over on 1st January 1905, at about the time of this photograph. The line to Wrexham General had been doubled in 1888. (Unknown)

108.   St. Marks Church dominates the skyline as 2-6-2T no. 41234 waits at platform 1, sometime
in the late 1950s. On the left is a train to Seacombe near Liverpool; the other is probably destined
for Chester Northgate. (Milepost 92½)

109.   The platforms were numbered from left to right (north to south) 1 to 5, only 3 and 4 being through ones. The original building is on the left. (Lens of Sutton coll.)

110.   No. 1432 has arrived with an autocoach from Ellesmere at platform 4 and is crossing to No. 3 from where it will depart. The date is 30th June 1956. (H.C.Casserley)

111.   A few minutes later and the train has completed its move over the crossover, then reversing into the platform. Empty stock is at platform 5, on the right. This and most of No. 4 were little used, hence the terminal condition of the lamp. (H.C.Casserley)

112.   St. Marks has vanished, but the goods shed is clearer (centre) in this view west on 19th May 1962. A brave attempt at floral decoration had been made with retired motor cycle tyres. The station was always less than generous with passenger provision. The ex-GCR signal box is in the left distance and it was moved to the present GCR in October 1988. It had 56 levers and was in use until August 1973. (P.J.Garland/R.S.Carpenter)

113.   Seen on the same day, 0-4-2T no. 1458 has its coach just in platform 4, after arrival from Ellesmere. The elderly folk are moving towards the barrow crossing, rather than the footbridge. (P.J.Garland/R.S.Carpenter)

114.   Having moved to platform 3, the crossing is obstructed, but there is time for leg crossing before the return journey. The goods yard in the background had a 5-ton crane and closed on 7th December 1964. (P.J.Garland/R.S.Carpenter)

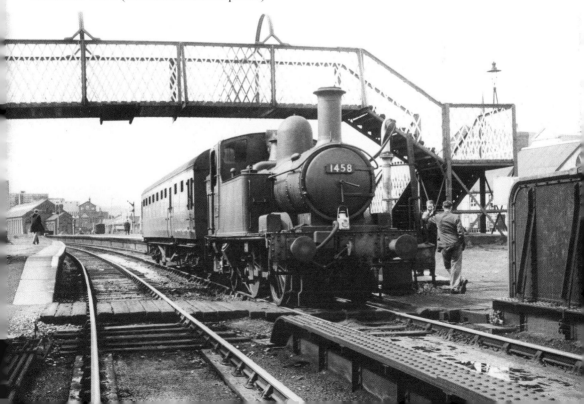

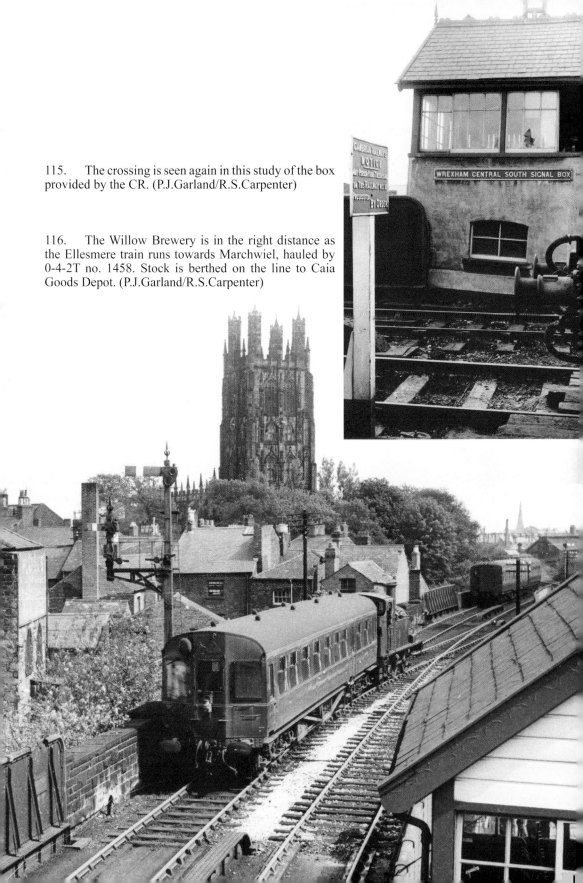

115.	The crossing is seen again in this study of the box provided by the CR. (P.J.Garland/R.S.Carpenter)

116.	The Willow Brewery is in the right distance as the Ellesmere train runs towards Marchwiel, hauled by 0-4-2T no. 1458. Stock is berthed on the line to Caia Goods Depot. (P.J.Garland/R.S.Carpenter)

WREXHAM CENTRAL SOUTH SIGNAL BOX

117.   The spread of DMUs in the 1960s brought such creations here. This example is on a Chester service. Class 142 units were introduced in October 1985. The station offices are on the right. (Colour-Rail.com.)

Wrexham	1923	1933
Passenger tickets issued	25245	16491
Season tickets issued	6	-
Parcels forwarded	3909	2133
General goods forwarded (tons)	48	13
Coal and coke received (tons)	-	54
Other minerals received (tons)	11	22
General goods received (tons)	46	48
Coal and Coke handled	-	71
Trucks of livestock handled	-	-

118.   The station was unstaffed after 7th February 1972 and this is terminal decline in both senses, early in 1998. A new terminus was built 400yds to the west and a major new shopping complex was created on the site. (S.C.Jenkins)

Great Western Railway.
CHESTER TO
WREXHAM
FIRST CLASS
Issued subject to the conditions
stated on the Cos. Time Bills. (HL)
Wrexham   Wrexham
5504

119.	The new station opened on 23rd November 1998 and was a prominent part of the new development. Two views from 29th June 2008 show well maintained facilities, although devoid of staff. (V.Mitchell)

120.	A three-car platform was provided on the single line to Wrexham General. Trains run to Bidston, where there are connections with the electric services on the West Kirby-Liverpool route. (V.Mitchell)

MP Middleton Press

EVOLVING THE ULTIMATE RAIL ENCYCLOPEDIA

Easebourne Lane, Midhurst, West Sussex.
GU29 9AZ   Tel:01730 813169

www.middletonpress.co.uk   email:info@middletonpress.co.uk
A-978 0 906520   B-978 1 873793   C- 978 1 901706   D-978 1 904474   E -978 1 906008

All titles listed below were in print at time of publication - please check current availability by looking at our website - *www.middletonpress.co.uk* or by requesting a Brochure which includes our *LATEST* RAILWAY TITLES also our TRAMWAY, TROLLEYBUS, MILITARY and WATERWAYS series